I was only Asking

Other books by Steve Turner
from Lion Publishing:

In the Beginning

The Day I Fell Down the Toilet

Dad, You're Not Funny

The Moon Has Got His Pants On

Poems

Steve Turner

I was only Asking

LION
Children's Books

Text copyright © 2004 Steve Turner
Illustrations copyright © 2004 Nigel Baines
This edition copyright © 2004 Lion Publishing

The moral rights of the author and illustrator
have been asserted

Published by
Lion Publishing plc
Mayfield House, 256 Banbury Road,
Oxford OX2 7DH, England
www.lion-publishing.co.uk
ISBN 0 7459 4821 9

First edition 2004
10 9 8 7 6 5 4 3 2 1 0

Acknowledgments
The poem 'Birth' on p. 42 was first published
in *Nice and Nasty* by Steve Turner,
(Marshall Morgan & Scott/Razor Books,1983).

A catalogue record for this book is available
from the British Library

Typeset in 12/16 Times
Printed and bound in Finland

Contents

Where Did I Come From?

Why Am I Here?

How Should I Live?

Why is There Something Rather Than Nothing?

Asking Questions

What? Why? Who?

If you want to ask a question
Think while on the loo.
Don't waste a precious moment:
      What? When? Who?

If you want to ask a question
Furrow up your brow.
Chew your pencil to the lead:
      When? Who? How?

If you want to ask a question
Wriggle in your chair.
Let the teacher see your face:
      Who? How? Where?

If you want to ask a question
Hold your hand up high.
Think of what you want to say:
      How? Where? Why?

If you want to ask a question
Choose the best you've got.
Wait until an answer comes:
       Where? Why? What?

If you want to ask a question
Trap it with your pen.
Nail it to the printed page:
       Why? What? When?

How to Daydream

Let your mind
Off its leash,
Let it chase, let it choose.
Let it sniff out ideas,
Let it mull, let it muse.

Don't command it to sit,
To lie down, to stay.
Let it rummage in reasons,
Let it roll, let it play.

Let your mind
Off its leash,
Let it stalk, let it track.
Let it lose its direction,
Let it find its way back.

Don't bark out instructions,
Just watch where it goes
As it follows its feelings,
Its hunches, its nose.

Puzzle

What has three legs, two heads,
Nine arms and can fly?

You don't know the answer?
Well, neither do I.

The Answer

The answer is
in a sealed envelope,
on a separate sheet,
at the back of the book,
on the tip of my tongue.

The answer is
hidden in the question,
blowing in the wind,
upside down,
hard to find.

The answer is
written in the heavens,
locked in a safe,
gone to the grave,
staring in your face.

The answer is

If You Don't Ask Questions

If you don't ask questions
you'll never know.
If you don't ask questions
you'll lose your way.
If you don't ask questions
you won't find the toilet.

If you don't ask questions
you won't discover.
If you don't ask questions
you'll be a stranger to yourself.
If you don't ask questions
someone will take your mind
and make it up for you.

If you don't ask questions
you won't find answers.
If you don't ask questions
you'll never know.

Who Knows?

'Now class! Who can tell me the answer?
Can anyone offer suggestions?'

Why is it that teachers are paid to know,
yet they're always asking us questions?

What Am I?

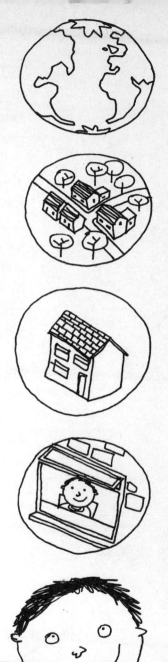

Where I'm Sitting

From space
I'm invisible.
From the clouds
I'm landscape.
From a tower
I'm an ant.
From a roof
I'm a speck.
From the street
I'm a shape.
From my door
I'm human.
From an armchair
I'm a person.
From where I'm sitting
I'm me.

What Am I?

What am I?
said the sky.

You're a mountain
for the sun to climb up,
an ocean
for clouds to float in,
a playground
for the wind to tumble into,
a balcony
for the moon to sit on.

You're a stage
for stars to dance on,
a race track
for planets to run around,
an empty space
for sound to travel across,
a distance
for me to stare into.

Dressing Up

Tin helmets, fedoras,
bowlers and caps.
I can be who I want
at the drop of a hat.

What About Me?

My grandad
saves raindrops from drowning.
My grandma
waves back at the sea.
Uncle Bill
puts snowflakes in freezers.
But no one
seems to care about me.

My father
likes talking to tulips.
My mother
hugs bushes and trees.
My sister
won't step on a daisy.
But no one
seems to care about me.

Aunt Freda
has made friends with spiders.
My brother
says he won't hurt a flea.
Cousin Faye
saves foxes from fox hounds.
But no one
seems to care about
                    me.

Rubbish

You may be rubbish at dancing,
or rubbish at hitting a ball
with a large wooden stick.
You may be rubbish at counting,
or rubbish at putting order
into the right words.
But you're not rubbish.
No one is rubbish.

empt

No one is a ball of paper,
or the curly skin of a potato.
No one is a twisted wheel,
or a fridge that no longer works.
No one chooses to live
on a scrap heap.
No one wants to be treated
like dirt.

You may be rubbish at inventing stories,
or rubbish at remembering
the punch lines of jokes.
You may be rubbish at skipping,
or rubbish at keeping your room
free from rubbish.
But you're not rubbish.

The voice that calls
and tells you that you're rubbish?
That's rubbish.
The voice in the middle of your head
that tells you that you're rubbish?
That's rubbish.

You may be rubbish at hearing
the music in your heart,
or rubbish at believing
all the wonders that you are.
But you're not rubbish.
No one is rubbish.

From a Tortoise Point of View

From a tortoise point of view
we are very strange creatures.
What happened to our front legs?
How do we stop from falling?
Why don't we carry our houses?

From a tortoise point of view
we live life too fast
and don't eat enough lettuce.
That's why we get stressed.
That's why we die young.

From a tortoise point of view
we are monsters:
huge upright standing animals
with naked backs,
who race around making fierce noises.

From a tortoise point of view
thinking never changes the world
and poetry makes no sense at all.

Who Am I?

Different

Two eyes.
Two ears.
One nose.
One mouth.
A skull.
Some skin.
Some hair.
Some teeth.
A tongue.

Everyone
exactly the same.

Every one
different.

My Name

I like my name.
It's not as great a sound
as a sea gull's cry
or the crash of a wave,
not as great a shape
as a snowflake
or a squirrel's tail,
but it's my sound, my shape,
and that's why I like it.

I like to see it on envelopes
and certificates.
I like to see it in newspapers
and magazines.
I like to hear it
called in the street.
I especially like to hear it
after the words
'And the winner is…'
and before the words
'… I love you.'

I feel close to my name
and my name
feels close to me.
I wear its syllables
like skin.

It's hard for me to imagine
what I would do
without my name.
How would I answer
such a simple question as
'Excuse me.
Who are you?'

The Me Bit

There's a me bit of me
Inside, somewhere deep,
That never takes time out
Or drops off to sleep.

My features it wears as
Its daily disguise.
It feels with my fingers
And looks through my eyes.

There's a me bit of me
That takes up no space.
You can't say you've found it
In heart, brain or face.

It won't show on X-rays.
You can't cut it out.
But it's there just the same –
Of that there's no doubt.

There's a me bit of me
That's just out of range.
To you it's a puzzle.
To me it seems strange.

It hides in a hollow
Inside my insides
And never gets smaller,
Or older, or dies.

When I'm with You

When I'm with Daisy
I go kind of crazy.
When I'm with Kai
I feel shy.
When I'm with Kitty
I feel sharp and witty.
But when I'm with you
       I'm just me.

When I'm with Sonny
I'm terribly funny.
When I'm with Vlad
I get sad.
When I'm with Billie
I start acting silly.
But when I'm with you
       I'm just me.

When I'm with Dwayne
I feel almost plain.
When I'm with Pam
I feel glam.
When I'm with Sally
I get rather pally.
But when I'm with you
       I'm just me.

Tell Me: Who Am I?

I'm found in many places.
I can't claim that I'm rare.
I rise from hidden caverns.
I fall down through the air.

You take me in a bottle.
I take you in a boat.
There's nothing you can teach me.
I teach you how to float.

My colour? I don't have one.
My shape? You just can't tell.
I have no stripes or patterns.
I have no taste or smell.

Sometimes you pray to find me.
Sometimes I spoil your days.
Sometimes you have to fight me.
Sometimes you give me praise.

Without me you would wither.
Without me you would die.
Without me plants would shrivel.
So tell me: who am I?

Answer: Water

End of Term Report

When they say you're 'making progress'
They mean you tend to cruise.
When they say you've 'got potential'
They mean it's never used.

When they say you've 'strong opinions'
They mean you're out of hand.
When they say 'a lively pupil'
They mean they'd like you banned.

When they say you're 'self-assured'
They mean you're over-proud.
When they say your 'gift is language'
They mean you're much too loud.

When they say you're 'easy-going'
They mean you're soft and woolly.
When they say you're 'born to lead'
They mean you're such a bully.

When they say you're 'most unique'
They mean you're out to lunch.
When they say you're 'entertaining'
They mean like Mr Punch.

When they say you're 'frank and honest'
They really mean 'uncouth'.
When they say you 'can't be taught'
Then, whoops, they've told the truth.

Cool

Mum and Dad wanted me to do well
In my studies at school
But all I wanted to be was
Cool.

Cool, not clever.
Cool, not nice.
Cool as a cucumber.
Cool as ice.

I wanted to walk into a room
Where everyone thought, WOW!
This guy is so up to date, so
NOW.

Cool, not clever.
Cool, not nice.
Cool as a cucumber.
Cool as ice.

But I didn't get points for being cool –
Image didn't get you good grades.
Learning wore a satisfied smile. Coolness,
Shades.

Where Did I Come From?

Heredity

From father's dad, a drooping lid,
From father's mum, these eyes.
From mother's mum, a shape of skull,
From mother's dad, my size.

From Dad himself, a long lean frame,
From Mum, this swarthy skin.
In me they're mixed together
With new things added in.

Now I'm a dad, I take these gifts;
I pass these markings on.
I see myself as I once was
In daughter and in son.

If I went back a thousand years
I'd find some folk, somewhere,
With this same shape, this look, this frame;
My eyes, my nose, my hair.

Where I Came From

If I had been found
beneath a gooseberry bush
I'd be green and round and hairy.
If I had been plucked
from a Christmas tree top
I'd be a Christmas tree fairy.

If I had been brought
in the beak of a stork
I'd be feathered
from fingers to toes.
If I had been sent
as a parcel, first class,
there'd be stamps all
over my nose.

If I had been made
out of sugar and spice
I'd melt into puddles of goo.
If I had been dropped
like a gift from the sky
my bum would have
broken in two.

If I had been picked
from a gardening patch
I'd stand like a plant in a vase.
If I had been sent
in an alien craft
I'd want to go back home to Mars.

But I wasn't picked
and I didn't fly
and I didn't fall on my bum.
I came from a place
of darkness and warmth
inside the inside of my mum.

Roots

It's a quiet job
being a root.
No one hugs you,
climbs you
or praises your
intricate ways.

Roots work
in the dark.
And it's hard work
tunnelling,
travelling,
finding nutrition.

But when
the storms come
it's our fingers
which cling.
When the drought comes
it's our lips
that drink.

Without us
the ground would crumble.
Without us
life would fall.

Everyone
needs roots.

Labels

There's a label inside
your shirt.
It tells you
who made it,
what size it is
and how to clean it.
There's a label
on your trainers.
There's even a label
in your pants,
although it's hard to read
once you've got them on.
But there's no label
on your body.
　There's no label
　　under your hair
　　　or on the sole
　　　　of your foot
to say where you came from,
who made you
and who to complain to
if something goes wrong.

My Town

No one famous
ever came from my town.
No great battle
was fought in my town.
On some small maps
you can't even see my town.
But I just love
the thought of my town.

In newspapers
you never read of my town.
No pop song has made
a claim on my town.
People say 'where?'
when I mention my town.
But I just love
the name of my town.

So wherever
I go I take my town.
Somewhere down deep
is a piece of my town.
I was brought up
by the folk of my town.
And I just love
the streets of my town.

God's Great Studio of Art

I'd love to have been a fly on the wall
In God's great studio of art
When he first had the idea for the world
And planned it all out on a chart.

I'd love to have heard the CRACK! and the POW!
As lightning crashed through his mind
To have seen the sweet smile of pleasure
That came with each sketch and each find.

I'd love to have seen the outlines and drafts
For the whale, the moon and the rose,
For the peacock, the dolphin, the tiger,
The elephant's ears and nose.

I'd love to have been a fly on the wall
In God's great studio of art
When he first had the idea for the world
And decided to give me a part.

Why Am I Here?

Snowmen

Snowmen have nothing to live for
Snowmen just stand still and stare
Snowmen are made for our pleasure
Snowmen just have to be there.

Snowmen don't get bored with standing
Snowmen get used to the cold
Snowmen were never once snowboys
Snowmen are born looking old.

Snowmen don't ask where they come from
Snowmen don't ask where they'll go
Snowmen can't be good or evil
Snowmen can only be snow.

Why Must I Live?

Why go to school?
To learn, child, to learn.
Why must I learn?
To work, child, to work.
Why must I work?
To eat, child, to eat.
Why must I eat?
To grow, child, to grow.
Why must I grow?
To live, child, to live.
Why must I live?
Er… to live, child, to live.

Birth

I didn't ask
to be born.
I wasn't even
there to ask.
When you are born
you can ask for
anything.
Almost anything.
You cannot ask
to be unborn.
If you do
there is very little
that can be done.
I didn't ask
to be born.
I was under age
at the time.
My parents had
to decide
on my behalf.
I'm glad that
I was born.
You have to be born
to be glad.

Why Am I Here?

Why am I here
rather than there
and why am I here at all?
Why am I bones
rather than sticks
and why not a box or a ball?

Why am I Steve
rather than Sam
and why not Jemima or Jim?
Why am I me
rather than you
and why am I not her or him?

Why am I skin
rather than leaf
and why not a rock or a cat?
Why am I he
rather than she
and why not just 'thingy' or 'that'?

All the Hours God Gives

I work all the hours God gives.
I work. All the hours – God gives.
I work all the hours. God gives.

God gives all the hours I work.
God gives. All the hours – I work.
God gives all. The hours? I work.

The hours God gives, I work.
The hours! God gives, I work.
I give God all the work hours.

The hours I give God all work.

45

Lazy Laura

Our Laura and work didn't mix well
Our Laura preferred life in bed
She was always looking for somewhere
To lay her languishing head.

A cushion, of course, could be comfy
A floor with a mat did the trick
An overcoat rolled in a bundle
Was good if the fabric was thick.

She could even sleep in the classroom
When the teacher said, 'Time to revise'
By laying her face in the textbook
And shutting her world-weary eyes.

A bus or a train was just perfect
For knocking off even more zzzzzzzzs
The rocking and rolling of transport
Would put her at once at her ease.

She thought of it all as 'just resting':
Re-charging the batteries inside
But the more time she spent chilling out
The more life at large passed her by.

She once dreamed of making a mark
An achievement that time wouldn't fade
In the end though her bed was her life
And sleep the lone mark that she made.

Be Careful with the World

Don't let it get too hot
Or crumble, rot or break
Be careful with the world
Don't scratch it by mistake.

Keep it clean and tidy
Improve its look and smell
Be careful with the world
Make sure it's working well.

Pass it on to others
Who haven't yet been born
Be careful with the world
Don't leave it wrecked and
    worn.

Love it like a best friend
Love it no matter what
Be careful with the world
It's the only world we've got.

How Should I Live?

Careers Advice

Johnson.
You're good at staring into space.
You can be an astronaut.

Patel.
You're good at copying other people's answers,
especially upside down.
You can be a magician.

Chivers.
You're good at making up excuses.
· You can be a politician.

Diggory.
You're good at shouting.
You can sell fruit and vegetables.

Matthews.
You're good at truancy.
You can be the space
into which Johnson stares.

The Golden Rule

If you like sweets
Give sweets away
If you like games
Let someone play
If you like toys
Make sure you lend
If you like fun
Tickle a friend.

If you like comfort
Wipe someone's brow
If you like help
Help someone now
If you like food
Feed the unfed
If you like sleep
Give up your bed.

If you like hugs
Hug someone new
If you like love
Then love them too
If you like freedom
Set someone free
If you like you
Try liking me.

The Love of Money

I don't love money.
It doesn't make much sense
To fall head over heels
In love with piles of pence.

I don't love money.
I'd rather kiss a goat
Than get into a clinch
With a twenty pound note.

I don't love money.
You don't know where it's been
And every time you hold it
You're looking at the queen.

I don't love money.
It's such a fickle friend
It promises the earth
But leaves you in the end.

Stubborn Stan

When Stan saw a sign that said SILENCE
Stan would suddenly shout
When a sign on a door said WAY IN
Stan would make his way out.

When Stan saw a sign that said PRIVATE
Stan would drive in with his car
When the captain announced, 'No smoking'
Stan would light up a cigar.

When the sign on the wire said DANGER
Stan touched it to show he was bold.
When AT REST was carved on his gravestone
Stan, at last, did as he was told.

Nothing for Me to Do

There's nothing for me to do.
I might as well be dead.
There's always something to do.
For example, make your bed.

There's nothing for me to do.
My life is unexciting.
Life is what you make it, dear,
Try some letter-writing.

There's nothing for me to do.
I don't even have the choice.
Why don't you phone your grandad?
He'd love to hear your voice.

There's nothing for me to do.
I can't stand it any more.
Why don't you help the homeless
Or feed the starving poor?

There's nothing for me to do.
I'm bored out of my mind.
There's something only you can do
That only you can find.

Spit

I don't have a talent for numbers
I don't understand English lit.
A baby could beat me at physics
But no one can beat me at spit.

I spit with the force of a bullet
I spit down the length of a hall
I can knock tin cans off a table
Or shoot it right over a wall.

If spitting was taught in the classroom
Then I'd be the top of the class
If exams in the art could be taken
Then I'd get an A-level pass.

I'd go on to do spitting at Cambridge
With a spit studies (honours) degree
And once I was a master of spit
I'd go for a spit PhD.

Yes, and then I'd spit for Great Britain
The Union Jack would unfurl
I'd spit myself through the Olympics
Outspitting the best in the world.

But spitting, although very clever
Is not a gift much in demand
In fact, when spitting is mentioned
It is mostly to say that it's banned.

What Life is Like

Life is like
a journey
with a beginning
and an end
      Or
Life is like a
traffic jam
that drives you
round the bend.

Life is like
a rose bed
with lots of
soft, red petals
      Or
Life is like
a rubbish tip
with rags and
twisted metals.

Life is like
a sweet dream
from which you never
want to wake
          Or
Life is like
a nightmare
with more scares than
you can take.

Life is like
a snowball
that gets bigger
as it's rolled
          Or
Life is like
an ice cream
that melts when
it is sold.

Life is like
A sunbeam
that brings light
to darkened places
            Or
Life is like
an autumn fog
that covers up
all traces.

Why is There Something Rather Than Nothing?

For Whom?

For whom do the stars twinkle
For whom does the moon shine down
For whom do the planets dance
For whom does the earth spin round?

For whom does the wind whistle
For whom does the thunder roll
For whom does the lightning crash
For whom do the raindrops fall?

For whom does the dolphin sing
For whom does the lizard crawl
For whom does the tiger roar
For whom does the peacock call?

For whom does the ocean swell
For whom does the forest grow
Who does the question hear
Who does the answer know?

Nothing Poem

This poem is about nothing
That's what it's about
Its subject is zero
Is *nada*, is nowt.

Like the time that existed
Before there was time
Like the hole in a Polo
The words in a mime.

Like what you said you'd been doing
The night you got caught
Like an absence of something
Like nought minus nought.

Like the number of dollars
In a bankrupted bank
Like a box without tricks
Like a screen that stays blank.

Like a snowman in summer
Like a tree when it sings
Like the sound that a moth makes
When beating its wings.

This poem is about nothing
That's what it's about
Its subject is zero
Is *nada*, is nowt.

NOTHING

What Could Have Been

There could have been
          nothing.
No earth, no planets.
No sun, no stars.
No you, no me.

With no sun
there'd be no light.
With no movement,
no sound.

With no eyes
the blackness
would not be seen.
With no ears
the silence
would not be heard.

With no minds
no questions would be asked,
no answers given.

Shadow

When the sun shines
I make a shadow.
It walks behind me,
it walks beside me,
it walks before me.
It never leaves me.
Having a shadow
means that I am.

Sunlight travels
for over 90 million miles,
then I get in the way.
People can look through me
but the sun can't.

If you have a shadow
it means that
you are.

63

What is Right or Wrong?

Seven Deadly Sinners

Tom, Tom the piper's son
Look after your own swine
Covet not that porky pig
For that live meat is mine.

Goosey, goosey gander
Your *anger* must be checked
Kicking people down the stairs
Can lead to broken necks.

Young man, you Knave of Hearts
I know you crave your cream
But eat the tarts in front of you
Don't *envy* what's the Queen's.

Little Boy, so-called Blue
You've turned into an oaf
Get up off your fat backside
Or else you'll die of *sloth*.

Naughty Georgie Porgie
I've got your moves well sussed
You don't love the girls you kiss
You're after them for *lust*.

Fine lady on a white horse
I've seen the way you ride
That flash of ring and toe bell
Is just a show of *pride*.

So then Mrs J. Spratt
I see you're into mutton.
Your problem's not with Jack now.
It's you. You great big *glutton*.

Differences of Opinion

When you shout you say you 'raise your voice'
When I do it, I'm 'going crazy'
When you stop work it's 'taking a break'
When I do it, I'm 'being lazy'.

When you're kind you say you're 'being nice'
When I do it, I'm 'acting wet'
When you fluff, you say things 'slipped your mind'
When I do it, I 'just forget'.

When you're proud you call it 'self-assured'
When I am, you say my 'head's too big'
When you eat too much you're 'filling up'
When I do it, I'm 'being a pig'.

When you confess you say you're 'facing facts'
When I do it, I'm 'giving in'
When you mess up you say 'it's a mistake'
When I do it, it's a 'sin'.

Conscience

Does a cloud feel bad
When it blots out the sun?
Does the wind feel sad
When it stops all our fun?
Does the snow feel pain
When it gives us a nip?
Does the sea feel sick
When it shakes up a ship?

Does a fox feel bad
When it fights with a cat?
Does a dog feel sad
When it corners a rat?
Does a fly feel pain
When it spreads a disease?
Does a mouse feel sick
When it chews up the cheese?

I feel sick
When I tell someone lies
I feel pain
When I don't apologize
I feel sad
When I say a word that's cruel
And I feel bad
When I break the golden rule.

Negligent Neville

Neville wasn't nasty.
He didn't scratch or bite.
He wasn't rude in public.
In fact, he was polite.
His shirts were always clean.
His teeth were always white.
The teachers gave him 'A's
For answers (always right).

The things that he did wrong
Were somewhat out of sight.
It wasn't that he stole
Or loved to shout and fight
But rather that he knew
The thing that would be right.
Yet, if it seemed too hard,
Would say 'maybe', 'I might'.

Example? Washing up.
He liked his dishes bright.
But would he wash a dish?
He wouldn't. You were right.
Example? Giving help
To others in their plight.
He saw the sick and poor
But wouldn't pray or write.

He never made his bed
Or dimmed the kitchen light.
He never cleaned the house
Or cooked his food at night.
He knew what he should do
To bring his mum delight
But always found excuses
However strange or slight.

Neville wasn't nasty.
He didn't scratch or bite
But never found the time
To do things that were right.
Too busy playing games
Too busy out at night
'Tomorrow I'll do something'
Of course. Exactly. Quite.

Moaning Minnie

Moaning Minnie always woke
in a mood that was most foul.
Her teeth were clenched in anger.
her brow became a scowl.

She moaned about the weather
(there was too much this or that).
She moaned about her figure
(she thought she was too fat).

She moaned about her mother
(she called her Mama Witch).
She moaned about her money
(she thought she should be rich).

She moaned about her teachers
(they didn't understand).
She moaned about her homework
(she thought it should be banned).

She moaned about her schoolmates
(she said they didn't care).
She moaned about her maths test
(she said it wasn't fair).

She moaned about her aunties
(they never ever phoned).
But she moaned the most of all
about those who always moaned.

Moses

Moses went up the mountain
Moses was covered in cloud
Moses came down with a list
Of things that were not allowed.

Moses said, 'These are the laws'
Moses said, 'You must obey'
The crowd said thank you to Moses
Then went on its own sweet way.

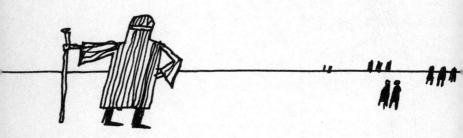

Nose-picking

Picking your nose is not evil
(Check in the laws sent to Moses)
The devil just doesn't have time
For tempting fingers up noses.

Nose-picking isn't illegal
It won't get you thrown into jail
It won't see you facing arrest
Or having to raise your own bail.

Picking your nose spreads no harm
The public are safe it is true
For the nose you typically pick
Is a nose belonging to you.

Nose-picking isn't a matter
That troubles the conscience at all
There's nothing to make you feel bad
In flicking or rolling a ball.

Picking your nose is bad manners
It's what we would term a taboo
It's rude, uncalled for, unsightly
It's something we try not to do.

What is Truth?

Fire

They say that fire is hot.
I think not.
I'm bold.
I say, 'Fire is cold.'

'Nonsense,' they say,
'Not so. Untrue.'
'Excuse me,' I say.
'Am I not entitled
to my own point of view?'

The Lie

When I was ten
I told a boy
that I had been born
in Los Angeles,
          California.

I had never even been
to America.
I had only ever
read about it in books
and seen it on TV.

But
Los Angeles,
          California,
sounded so much more exciting
than Napton-on-the-Hill,
          Warwickshire.

Help Line

Welcome to the help line
Your call is in a queue,
You'll have to hang on in there
Before we get to you.

To help us in the meantime
Please listen to my voice
Then press the keys I tell you
To make your final choice.

Press number one for queries
We'll see what we can do
And anyone with questions
Instead, press number two.

If you think you need some help
Then pick the number three.
If you're looking for advice
Then number four's your key.

Please touch the number five
If you find you're in a fix.
If you're totally confused
Then press the number six.

Welcome to the help line
Your call is in a queue
But if you have a problem
There's nothing we can do.

I was bald when I started this call...

Hitting is Not Really Hitting

Hitting is not really hitting;
it's pushing
with a little more clout.
White lies are not really lies;
they're truths
with some bits taken out.

Nasty is not really nasty;
it's telling
facts people can't face.
Shouting is not really shouting;
it's talking
with more volume and bass.

Cheating is not really cheating;
it's taking
what you think you deserve.
Gossip is not really gossip;
it's sharing
some things that you've heard.

Stealing is not really stealing;
it's finding
what fell off a shelf.
Naughty is not really naughty;
it's just being
true to yourself.

What is Truth?

The truth
  is
what's what.
A lie
  is
what's not.

Washing Our Hands

Sometimes we wash our hands
When guilty of a crime
Quick thinking in the bathroom
Can buy us extra time.

Sometimes we wash our hands
To lift a stubborn stain
Clues that might convict us
Go swirling down the drain.

Sometimes we wash our hands
To bring things to a halt
To let the public know
It's really not our fault.

Sometimes we wash our hands
To get a brand new start
Wanting new scrubbed fingers
And not a new scrubbed heart.

How Do We Know?

Mother's Instinct

My mother couldn't see into the future.
She could see into the present,
which was much worse.
She'd say,
'You're up to something.'
I'd say,
'How do you know?'
and she'd say,
'I can just tell.'

I reckon that she could
read my mind.
I'd have to think in another language
to confuse her.
Sometimes she would have
what she called a 'strange feeling'
that I was misbehaving
even though I was miles away.

It was like having eyes
in the back of my head.
My mother's eyes.

I once asked her about
this uncanny ability.
'How do you know?'
I said.
'You just know,' she said.
'When you're a mother
you just know.'

How Do You Know?

My name is Stephen
How do you know?
That's what they call me
How do you know?
My mother told me
How do you know?
I was there, listening
How do you know?
I can remember
How do you know?
I can remember
How do you know?
I know that I know
that I know that I know
and that's how I know
that I know.

The earth is round
How do you know?
I've seen a picture
How do you know?
It was in a book
How do you know?
I still have the book
How do you know?
I can remember
How do you know?
I can remember
How do you know?
I know that I know
that I know that I know
and that's how I know
that I know.

'Life is like an ice cream van,'
My granny used to say.
I meant to ask her what she meant
But then she passed away.

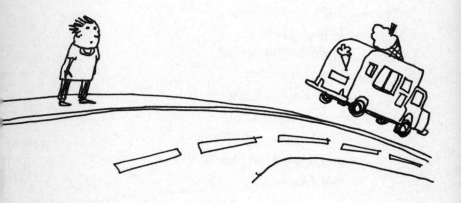

Elvis

Elvis didn't really die
He bought a council flat
He was sick of all the fame
And sick of being fat.

He swapped his studded costumes
For overalls and jeans
Waved goodbye to Memphis
And came to Milton Keynes.

He's got a job at Tesco's
He stacks the shelves at night
He says it keeps him busy
And keeps him out of sight.

There among the cans of beans
He found his peace of mind
Being nothing but a stacker
Stacking all the time.

BEANS

Loch Ness Monster

I often wonder
about the Loch Ness Monster.
If it really is there,
where does it hide?
Does it lie on the lake floor
or live in a side cave
with interesting rooms?
Is it male or female,
married or single?
Do small fish scatter
when it swims their way?

I think about the times
it pushes its head
through the water's surface.
Why so infrequently?
Doesn't it like what it sees?
Is the fresh air and sunlight
as frightening to it
as the dark depths of the loch
are to us?

I imagine it returning to its family
and telling them about
the strange world upstairs;
telling them about the small monsters
who point black boxes with glass eyes
that can steal your soul
in a click and a flash.

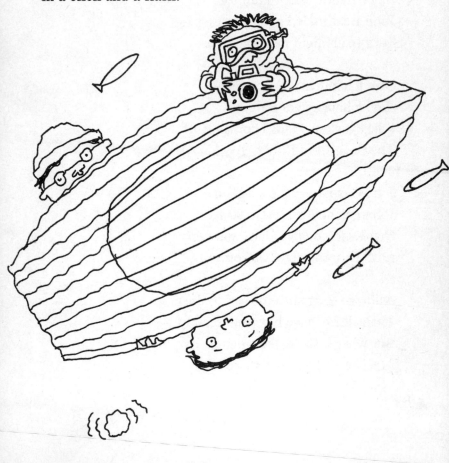

Where Are We Going?

Oundle Directory 1830

Thomas Wyman, he built wheels
Mary Ladds made them too
John Beal traded guns and clocks
Tom Britchfield mended shoes.

Sam Chapman was the baker
Rev. Isham spoke for God
Baskets came from Thomas Ruff
The meat from Robert Todd.

Job Watson was the surgeon
John Quenby carved in stone
Ben Knibb dealt in hats and caps
Lord Lilford stayed at home.

All have long since turned to dust
Their deeds have blown like straw.
But when I speak their names like this
I feel them live once more.

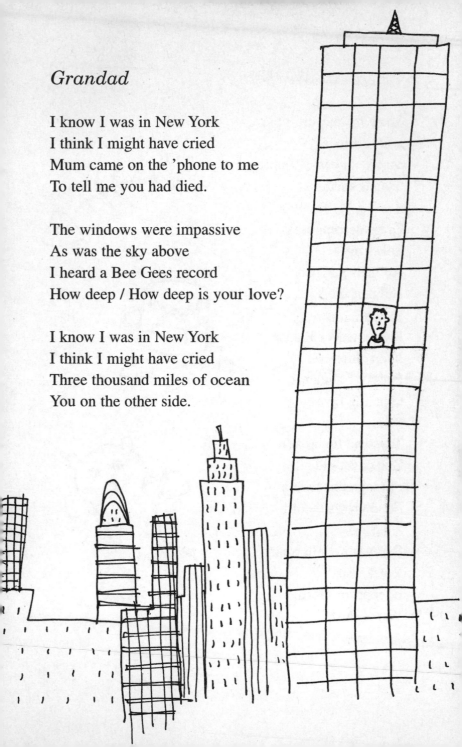

Grandad

I know I was in New York
I think I might have cried
Mum came on the 'phone to me
To tell me you had died.

The windows were impassive
As was the sky above
I heard a Bee Gees record
How deep / How deep is your love?

I know I was in New York
I think I might have cried
Three thousand miles of ocean
You on the other side.

Where Are We Going?

The cliff tops crumble
Land shrinks
Mountain peaks topple
Islands sink.

Grass decomposes
Lakes dry
Animals perish
Humans die.

Monuments collapse
Paint chips
Pottery fragments
Clothing rips.

Toys end up broken
Books get old
Photographs fade out
Food grows mould.

Everything falls apart
Rots, rusts
Except for the air
Water, dust.

At One I Thought...

At one I thought twos
  were so grown up
At two I thought threes were too large
At three I thought fours
  ran the world
At four I thought fives were in charge.

At five I thought sixes
  gigantic
At six I thought sevens were tall
At seven I thought eights
  were so clever
At eight I thought nines knew it all.

At nine I thought tens
  had it sorted
At ten I thought elevens had changed
Every age that I've been
  seemed quite normal
Yet the age after that seemed strange.

Pen, Ink, Paper, Glue

Pen, ink,
Paper, glue,
What do you think
You'll turn into?

Ink, glue,
Paper, pen,
I'll turn nine first
And then turn ten.

Cat, dog,
Parrot, pig,
What will you do
When you get big?

Dog, parrot,
Pig, cat,
A little bit of this,
A little bit of that.

Spoon, bowl,
Saucer, cup,
What will you be
When you grow up?

Bowl, saucer,
Cup, spoon,
I don't know yet
But I will do soon.

When I Grow Up

When I grow up
     I'm going to:

Run down a corridor
Jump down a stair
Speak with my mouth full
Uncomb my hair.

Leave all my broccoli
Undo my lace
Shout in the classroom
Dirty my face.

Stare at every stranger
Swing on a gate
Pick my nose in public
Go to bed late.

Gain a reputation
Break all my bones
Lose all the friends I've had
Live all alone.